Violin I

Violin I

SCHIRMER'S LIBRARY OF MUSICAL CLASSICS

F. MAZAS

Duets

For Two Violins

G. SCHIRMER, Inc.

DISTRIBUTED BY

7777 W. BLUEMOUND RD. P.O. BOX 13819 MILWAUKEE, WI 53213

Six Duets for 2 Violins.

The pupil must retain any given position until the fingering changes.

VIOLIN I.

F. MAZAS Op. 39, Book I.

VIOLIN I.

MINUETTO.
Andantino. (♩ = 96.)

RONDO.
Allegretto. (♩ = 100.)

12161

Violin II

SCHIRMER'S LIBRARY
OF MUSICAL CLASSICS

F. MAZAS

Duets

For Two Violins

G. SCHIRMER, Inc.

DISTRIBUTED BY

HAL•LEONARD®
CORPORATION
7777 W. BLUEMOUND RD. P.O. BOX 13819 MILWAUKEE, WI 53213

Six Duets for 2 Violins.

The pupil must retain any given position until the fingering changes.

VIOLIN II.

F. MAZAS. Op. 39, Book I.

⊓ Down-bow.
V Up-bow.

Printed in the U. S. A.

VIOLIN II.

4

VIOLIN II.

VIOLIN II.

Allegro non troppo.(♩=132)

2.

12161

VIOLIN II.

Andantino. (♪ = 112.)

sempre dolce

restez
retain

dim.

A

B

C

restez

dim.

p

POLACCA.
Tempo moderato. (♩ = 88.)